WILDLIFE POEMS

by

Kate Williams

Published by Kate Williams, 2009
ISBN: 9780953842841

Design by Martin Williams
Printed by CPI Antony Rowe Ltd, Chippenham
More info: www.~~freewebs.com/kate-williams~~
poemsforfun.wordpress.com

Contents

Poems

	page
Grumpillas	1
Jungle Jitters	2
Monkeying Around	3
Leap	4
Lionel the Lion	4
Hyena Laughter	5
Jaguars and Jaguars	6
Summer Heat	7
Parrot Talk	8
Stripes through the Streaks	9
Down the Jungle Path	10
Back up the Track	11
Crocodile Doze	12
My Pet Croc	12
If You Were A Giraffe	13
Zebra Crossing	14
Aunty Jean	15
Hippos and Haikus	16
Never Fight with Rhino-Might	17
What Do Kangaroos Like?	18
Haiku on a Hide-Winder	19
Desert Danger	19
Gold and Grand	20
Polar Pyjamas	21
Colder... Warmer...	22
Dance of the Penguins	23

November Seaside	24
Voice Beyond the Shore	25
Ocean of Possibilities	26
Tropical Fish	27
Mistress of the Sea	28
Albatross	29
Sea-bed Secrets	30
Sea Shore Sores	30
The Heron	31
Swan of the Night	31
Puddle Pictures	32
Quackerboxes	33
Nature Walk	34
Ripply Riddle	35
Slugs in the Garden	36
What is a Slug for?	37
What on Earth?	38
Butterfly Friend	39
The Good Life	40
Mike and the Wasp	41
Ant Talk	42
Spider-phobia	43
Wound-Up Woodlouse	44
Drifting, Drifting	45
Lady-bird-y	46
Not Quite	47
Life Sentence	48
Beyond the Patio Doors	48
Who's There?	49
Bad Feeling	50
The Intruder	51
Nightfall Fantasy	52

In a Forest Far Away 53
Master of the Midnight Hour 54
Tip-toe-ing 55
Rabbit Riot 56
Hawk Hazard 57
The Owl 58
Squirrelbatics 59
Dozy Toes 60
Small Figure, Big Digger 61
The Wind and the Wood 62
While Gales Push 63
I'd Be Full of Charm 64
Sleeping Willow 64
Freak in the Fog 65
Below the Snow 66
Anticipating 67
Busy Blackbird 68
Cocky Cock-Robin 68
Hide-and-Sleep 69
Sunny Sunday in the Park 70
What Sort of Green is a Sun-Lit Leaf? 71
Birds Over Buildings 72
Glad I'm Not a Human 73
Daydreaming 74
In My Next Life 75

Index of Creatures
Index of Weather & Whereabouts
Riddle Answers

Grumpillas

Sulky so-and-sos, gorillas, aren't they!
If you ever pass one, hunched on crossed legs,
don't try and pass the time of day.

Smile, and he'll stare back.
Chat, and he'll chew back.
Sing, and he'll sigh back.
Shout, and he'll shrug back.
Leave, and he'll hurl a banana at your back.

At least they don't go in for tomatoes
or raw eggs.

Jungle Jitters

Between the leaves,
lids blink,
between the ferns,
lashes wink,
between the vines,
eyes burn,
between the mish-mash-mesh of twines,
two turn...
and I turn too!

Monkeying Around

Trampolining, tree to tree!
Bungee-jumping – look at me!
Backwards, sideways, upside down,
doing the dare-devil,
acting the clown!

Swinging, leaping...
whoops – just missed...
saved myself with a mid-air twist!

Hanging down by my little toe...
oh...
and meeting two eyes
below.

Leap

GUSH	of power
	of dare
FLUSH	of colour
	of air
BRUSH	of whisker
	of hair
RUSH	of leopard -
	bush scare!

Lionel the Lion

Lionel the Lion
lies lazing in his lair,
Mabel, his lion bride,
lying at his side,
and a limb
lying on the table.

Hyena Laughter

Hyena laughter spiked the night,
wild, weird, full-moon-mad,
and went
echoing,
echoing,
echoing,
echoing...

echoing
over the scorch-black scrub,
over the torch-bright eyes,
echoing
over the dead-still trees,
over the tread-light spies,
echoing
over the quaking land,
over the shaking skies,

wild, weird, full-moon-mad,
echoing,
echoing,
echoing,
echoing...

Jaguars and Jaguars

People think I have four wheels,
and another one, too, to sit behind.
They think I go *Brmm, brmm! Toot, toot!*
But they'll find,
should they meet me one dark night,
that I'm a jag of a junglier kind –
not that *I'd* mind,
but they might.

Summer Heat

Pound
Pound
Pound
Pound

Pumping the air
Thumping the ground
Wringing out scents
Cracking up sounds
Grilling green brown
Baking lakes down

Pound
Pound
Pound
Pound

Pounding the dizzy day round

Parrot Talk

Hello, parrot! Can you talk?

Can you talk?

Of course I can talk. I'm human.

I'm human!

No you're not. You've got a beak.

You've got a cheek!

Hey, I do the rhymes round here!
I'm the poet. You're just a parrot.
You can only squawk.

Talk, talk, talk!

Oh, fly away!

Fly away!

I wish I could!

You can only walk!
You can only walk!
You can only walk!

Stripes through the Streaks

Through the streaks of stalk and stem,
through the strands of twine and twig,
stripes are sliding.

Black through gold, gold through black,
slanting strips through slatted slits,
velvet limbs through woven looms,
wild-cat stripes through wild-wood streaks
are sliding,
sidling.

Down the Jungle Path

Down the track Old Stripy slunk,
peeking here, poking there,
round the roots and shoots and trunks,
gawping with his green-eyed glare.

Down our garden path he crept,
scouting for young, sweet prey,
slinking where he thought we slept,
poised to capture and slay.

All day he poked his nose our way,
while we poked our tongues at him,
for we were at play in our hide-away
throughout this interim.

Back up the Track

Back, back, up the track,
head down, tail slack,
grumble-faced and humble-paced,
we watched Old Stripy go;

watched him slowly double back,
jilted from his juicy snack;
back, back, up the track,
slow as his legs would go;

watched his gown of brass and black
shrink and sink up the twilight track;
watched the fading of our foe
into the sundown glow.

Then we grabbed our bedrooms back.

Crocodile Doze

Sleeping,
floating,
legs out flat...
peeping,
gloating –
who's he looking at?

My Pet Croc

My croc's quite fantastic –
mean, creepy,
spikes down his back,
green scales, sharp nails,
slap-tail and that.

But he does a squeak instead of a snap.
That's why he's not fantastic, only quite.
He's got no bite.
But then, he's plastic.

If You were a Giraffe

If you were a giraffe,
with a drain-long, crane-strong, swing-along neck,
would you just eat leaves?
I wouldn't.
I'd be a spy.

I'd peep over fences ten feet high,
and snoop through windows up in the sky,
and peer into aeroplanes flying by,
spying all day with my aerial eye
to catch all the crooks and thieves.

Well, I'd do *something* anyway.
I wouldn't just eat leaves.

Zebra Crossing

Ever seen
a zebra crossing
a zebra crossing?

Nor me.

Ever seen
a zebra crossing
a wild savannah track?

I have.
He was after my snack.

Aunty Jean

Aunty Jean, Aunty Jean,
sat on an elephant, grand as a queen,
sat in her brand new blouse and skirt,
beaming down at Uncle Birt.

Aunty Jean, poor Aunty Jean,
sat on her elephant, stiff and serene,
till it sucked at a bucket of animal dirt,
twizzled its trunk, and gave her a squirt.

Least you're not hurt, said Uncle Birt,
and the clothes 'll clean, the clothes 'll clean.
He scrubbed her shirt and brushed her skirt,
but the elephant flushed her in between.

I'll never be clean! cried Aunty Jean.
At least you had your ride, Birt tried.
*But I'll never again feel clean inside -
never feel Queen!*
Birt sighed.

Then the elephant squirted Birt.
Poor Uncle Birt.

Hippos and Haikus

A rhinoceros
fits neatly in a haiku,
but a hippopot...

(A haiku has 3 lines, with five syllables in the first and last, and seven syllables in the middle. There are three more haiku in this book.)

Never Fight with Rhino-Might

A rhino is like dynamite:
disturb her, and she'll ignite.

What's more, she's large,
and expects your respect.

So don't stand in her way
and expect her to say
Excuse me!
or even *Oi, shift!*
or even to barge.

Expect her to charge.

What Do Kangaroos Like?

Kangaroos don't just like to jump.
They like to land too –

plump on top of your car windscreen,
or your picnic rug,
or your scones and cream,
or the lemonade jug,
or the long, red carpet rolled out for the Queen
when Her Majesty visits to the zoo,
or over the wall, past the cameras and all,
to give her a hug and a *How-do-you-do?*
as she steps from the back of her black limousine,
one foot on her shoe.

They like the high life, kangaroos do.

Haiku on a Hide-Winder

The sly side-winder
rides the sliding, hiding sand.
Now you see her, now...

Desert Danger

Slinking
through the heat
comes a desert
spy
winking
at my feet
with
oval
evil
eye

Gold and Grand

As the great yolk arches to the far horizon -
too bright to cast bare eyes on -
the camels march, dreaming of night,
looking neither left nor right.

Bearing up as the sun bears down,
they tread the parched, scorched ground,
gold and grand as the rolling sand
that shapes the land around.

On and on the creatures lurch,
each with a rider perched,
till day gives way, at last, to night,
and moonshine's egg-shell white.

Polar Pyjamas

Pillow-puffy,
cushion-fluffy,
the dozy cubs twitch sleepy feet,
cuddly, snugly, cosy and nice
between blanket and sheet
of snow and ice.

Colder... Warmer...

Slipping through ice is not nice –
especially into a pool.

Slipping through snow isn't cold, though,
and zipping down it – that's cool!

'Course a walrus wouldn't think twice.
He'd find it all warm and nice,
though he's most at ease
at sub-zero degrees,
and picks arctic dips as a rule.

Dance of the Penguins

Step
hop
        waddle
        stop
                blink
                scratch
                        think.

Step
hop
        wobble
        skid
                dash
                splash
                        sink.

November Seaside

Ever been to the seaside in November?
A British seaside?
You'd remember:
it's grim.

The sea looks grey as iron,
and hard as iron to lie on -
a great iron wedge.

You wouldn't want to swim.
The chill drills through your toes
just standing at the edge.

Ever tried it in December?
Loud as a lion?
High as a ledge?
Sharp as shark-teeth through your shoe?

I'll leave that to you.

Voice Beyond the Shore

Behind the splashes and giggles and screams
I can hear the ocean humming.

Beyond the picnics and rustling ice creams
I can hear her singing, sighing.

But from where, where, is her lullaby coming?
From far or near?
Or down deep?

From everywhere and nowhere,
like in dreams.

All I know is the ocean is humming,
like a giantess half asleep.

Ocean of Possibilities

Dolphin! Dolphin!
Where? Where?
(Rush to port-hole: stare, stare.)
See his head there?
That's a rock.
See that somersault?
That's a wave.
See the silver-blue flash of his fin!
That's spray!
Who can say?
(Both stare, stare...)

Tropical Fish

Tropical fish don't just shine:
they speak with their shine.

They shout from below
through their glorious glow:
These colours are mine!
These waters are mine!

Tropical wish.

Mistress of the Sea

Up she comes,
mistress of the sea,
ploughing the weighty water,
the slow centuries.

Here she comes,
worldly whale,
riding the rolling miles,
the rolling millennia.

There she goes,
forever at the helm,
sailing the oceans of mystery,
of history.

On she flows,
past you and me,
through her maritime, all-time
realm.

Albatross

Lonely ocean bird
surfing the sunset's glow -
so bright,
so white,
so graceful,
so grand,
so silent,
so strong,
solo!

Sea-bed Secrets

Like nocturnal eyes
glimmering in gloomy woods,
deep sea shoals shimmer.

Sea Shore Sores

Sting of jellyfish,
nip of crab, bone spike, shell stab,
shingle tingle – ouch!

The Heron

I saw him sit beside the lake,
one dark and frosty morning.

I saw him sit beside the lake,
then arc across without warning.

Swan of the Night

Lake-swimming swan,
late-swimming swan,
she'd sail while the pale moon shone.
But at dawn's first light
she'd quickly take flight,
and from morn till night she'd be gone.

Puddle Pictures

In every puddle
lies a picture in a muddle,
wibble-wobbling upside down.

Then the puddle dries
and the picture dies
and all you can see is
brown.

Quackerboxes

Quacker-chat-chatter!
Quacker-chat-splatter!
Quick – something's swimming our way!

Quick-quack-attack!
It's a tasty snack!
First fish platter of the day!

Dip down swish
to fish-dish-delish
through swirly, whirly, weedy waterway...

Then flip-flap-back –
back to quacker-chat –
So, as I say...
Quack-quack-quack!

Nature Walk

Slid in sludge,
flat on belly.
Stank my scarf,
sank a wellie.
Friends all laughed,
called me *Smelly*,
sent me off to have a bath
while they watched telly.

Ripply Riddle

Above the rings of the pool
tiny jewels flit,
sun-lit,
on silk-spun wings,
enjoying the cool.

Slugs in the Garden

Slugs
slowly go nowhere for hours
while we're watching,
then
wholly devour our flowers
while we're watching
TV.

What is a Slug For?

When I asked myself what a slug was for,
at first I wasn't quite sure.

I knew what it *wasn't* for, at least:
it wasn't for feasting on flowers – the beast!
But it must have a role in the world as a whole,
I thought, however obscure.

Slug, I thought, slug... what on earth was it for?
I knew that it rhymed with *hug* and with *mug*
(not that you'd want to give one a hug,
or let it go sliding down into your mug),
but what was it *for*?

It rhymed, too, with *bug*, I noticed next day
(which, after all, it is in a way)
and with *plug, rug* and *jug*
and with *snug, tug* and *lug*
and with *pug* (as in dog) and with *ugggh!*
and with smug, drug, lug, shrug, dug and,
for a sluggish car, *chug*.

continued...

Fine! But what was it actually *for* -
this squelchy, slobbery blob on the floor,
slumped on its sucker-foot plump in the way,
with nothing to do and nothing to say?

What, in the great scheme of things, was it for -
this featureless creature all covered in slime,
with no aim in life but flower-bed crime?
Something, surely, very obscure!

I puzzled and pondered a trail-long time...
till I suddenly saw:
a slug is for rhyme.

What on Earth?

Long
round
underground
squirmy like an eel
bird's meal

Butterfly Friend

Tiny gift-wrap bow
lifting
drifting
lifting

sky-high
meadow-low
sky-high

lifting
drifting
lifting

lifting me over the hedgerow
over the rainbow
over tomorrow

The Good Life

Lucky snail, having that house!

No locking up and taking a key!
No racing there and back in a day,
or staying overnight in a 'B.& B.'!
Free to roam, yet always at home!
Hey - and no bills to pay!

I'm envious...
in a way.

Mike and the Wasp

Mike's like: *Yikes!*
And the wasp's like: *Zzzzz!*
And I'm: *Get on y' bike, Mike!*
And Mike's like: *How?*
And the wasp's like circling
And Mike's doing swipes.
And I'm: *just get cycling!*
But Mike's like: *Ow!*

Ant Talk

Up a bit!
Down a bit!
Round the stones and in between!
Keep the cheese above the grit!
Things we do to please that queen!

Rest a bit!
Test a bit!
Farmhouse Cheddar – best I've seen!
Let's just sit and eat a bit,
before it's seized for the royal tureen!

(Researchers say ants 'talk' with their antennae, and that worker ants 'speak' in a different tone from their queen.)

Spider-phobia

I have a fear of spiders.
Have you?

It's the way they appear, as if from nowhere,
then disappear,
anywhere –
round your chair...
up your back...
down your hair...
underwear...
the dish on the dining-room table...
the toe of your shoe...

That's the scare:
never knowing what they'll do,
or
w
h
e
r
e.

Wound-Up Woodlouse

Here comes my little woodlouse,
rolling along the wall!
Tiny, wind-up, clockwork toy
on a tiny roller-ball.

Boink!
He's bumped my finger-tip.
Boink!
He's met my thumb.
Boink!
And now he's taken fright -
rolled up in a ball...

Not quite clockwork after all.

Drifting, Drifting

Drifting through the air,
legs a-dangle,
skirting nettles, gorse, brambles,
just drifting.

Drifting in your path,
legs a-tangle,
brushing your knee, arm, hair,
just drifting.

Silver-grey as the evening light,
half in, half out of sight,
thread-legs, web-wings, pin-thin body,
just drifting.

You can wave, clap, shout, jump,
run at the thing with a stick,
but the daddy-longlegs has never a care,
a-sail in the fairytale August air,
just drifting.

Lady-bird-y

Speckledy-dotty,
dottledy-specky,
freckledy-spotty,
spottledy-frecky,
metally-bright,
petally-light,
whoopsy-daisy
beetle-y-thing.

Not Quite

A moth is not quite a butterfly -
not quite as beautiful or bright.
But then, a moth is many things not quite.

For a start, his wings aren't right -
part tapestry, part bark of tree:
not dead, yet not alive - quite.
And he's never asleep, nor quite awake,
unless you give him a shake -
that'll send him whirring! Or it might.

He stirs those wings in the dark of night -
or at least, in the murky half-light,
and whirls around in the wild outside -
or inside - he can never quite decide.
He might drop in without invite
and head for your bedside reading light -
or just to one side -
and settle down for the night.

There's nothing black or white about a moth,
save that he *is* a moth, and not a myth -
quite.

Life Sentence

The mayfly may
fly for one May day.

Beyond The Patio Doors

Fox creeps
Mouse peeps
Toad sleeps
Frog l - e - - a - - - p - - - - s
Dad snores

Who's There?

You open your eyes:
it's dead of night.

All is dark,
except a slice of lamp-light
on the window sill.
All is silent and still.

Actually, not quite.
There's somebody around.

Someone's making a snorting sound...
outside, down by the shed...
someone big and black,
with a moonbeam down his head,
rubbing, scrubbing, sniffing the ground...

A badger, sorting a snack!

Back to bed.

Bad Feeling

Hole in trousers
hole in frock
hole in shoe sole
hole in sock
hole in hall floor
hole in house
hole in next-door
indigestion in mouse

The Intruder

Rat-a-tat-tat!
Rat-a-tat-tat!

Is that a little mouse?

No, I'm a rat,
come from the sewer, splish, splatter, splat,
to make your house my new habitat.

I'm bringing my germs and diseases and that
up from the drain to your under-floor flat.
In half a min. I'll be up for a chat -
and a bite from your bin to keep myself fat!

That's ten seconds flat to get rid of your cat,
or beware:
I'm a splat-a-cat rat!

Nightfall Fantasy

Head of mouse,
teeth of rat,
vampire wings
that whip and slap,
eyes that don't see,
ears that do:
donkey's ears that stare at you,
hamster's body,
piglet's nose,
gymnast's legs
that hang from toes,
voice - a pixie's tiny wail,
hobby - night-flight:
fairytale.

In a Forest Far Away

Moonlit:

a zillion silver snow-flakes, in spangles,
a mesh of silver twiglets, in tangles,
a swathe of silver tree trunks, at angles,
a pair of twitching triangles,
wolf-grey.

Unlit:

?

Master of the Midnight Hour

Expert at the soft tiptoe,
champion of speed,
braver of the winter snow,
his hungry cubs to feed,
chief of every glen and glade,
guard of every trail,
shadower of every shade
that flits round hill and vale,
dancing partner to the night,
groom to Dark's sly bride,
prince of starlight,
star of moonlight,
king of the countryside.

Tip-toe-ing

Through the woods
hopp-
ing,
stopp-
ing,
tip-
toe-
tread-
ing,
check-
peck-
swivel-head-
double-check-
peck-
ing,
dread-
dread-
dread-
ing
the spring of the Red Fox King.

Rabbit Riot

The bunnies jump high in the clover,
skipping, darting about,
rioting till the day's over,
till the Goldilocks rays run out,

then quietly dip down a hole
as Black-Socks starts her patrol.

Hawk Hazard

Watch out for the Bull's-Eye Spy!
Look at his shadow on the ground!
Heed its warning; feel its chill!
Hide, little thing, and don't be found!

He's hanging square above you in the sky,
poised there on wings too fast for sound,
dead-straight, dead-set, dead-sure, dead-still...

Get underground!

The Owl

As I freed a moth from my window,
I heard a screech-owl below,
down in the dip where the furry things hide:
where hill meets hooded wood.

I heard its shriek rip the night,
tearing the air like a bite,
slicing the dark down its deadly glide,
splicing that hide-away hood.

My moth went riding the star-glow,
light as a leaf from the wood.

Squirrelbatics

Trees in the breeze,
squirrels in the trees,
springing-clinging-swinging
from trapeze to trapeze.

Dozy Toes

What's
roly-poly
dozy-cosy
slowly-slowly
teeny-toes-y
creepy-crawly
Mind the taxi!
small-y-ball-y
nearly splatsy

?

Small Figure, Big Digger

For a shy little figure,
he's a sly, fickle digger,
that mole in his mobile hole!

Ploughing up the lawn
from dusk till dawn,
leaving us a muddy mess to see!

And he's deep under cover
by the time we discover,
plotting his next graffiti spree.

So where's tonight's to be?
Park? Pitch? Marquee?
All we know is: he'll escape scot-free.

The Wind and the Wood

All day the hurricane hammered the trees,
bending them into beggars,
whipping them till they wailed and moaned
and sank to their creaking knees.

Hour after hour he lashed the poor wood,
snapping his trembling twigs,
bashing his branches, thrashing his leaves,
as only a bully-boy could.

But when dusk fell, the wind went to bed,
and the trees stretched tall again,
and the wood looked grand as the King of the Land
with his green crown back on his head.

While Gales Push

Beneath the bush
lies a lump of a toad,
slumped in slumber,
safely stowed
in leaf-gold skin
and leaf-mould shawl,
as the gusts begin
and the cold rains fall.

While gales push
and water streams,
the toad in his bush stump
dreams.

I'd Be Full of Charm

Let the sky be dark and wild,
the high peaks, stark and stony;
let the moors roll mile on mile,
bleak and bare and lonely –
I'd be forever sweet and calm,
meek, mild, full of charm –
roaming my home with a sleepy smile,
if I was a Dartmoor pony...

if.

Sleeping Willow

Statue
riding the rolling sky,
still as a swan on a lake,
buds deep-chilled
till time comes to wake.

Freak in the Fog

Through the thick fog, whirling, whirling,
comes some creature, rolling fast.

Evil spirit? Wizard? Witch?
Giant grizzly? Jump in ditch!

Through the fog, uncurling, uncurling,
comes my teacher, strolling past.

Below the Snow

Still, white, winter world;
beneath it creatures tightly curled.

Thick, steep sweep of snow;
ticking hearts deep down below.

Chilling, killing crystal layer;
below, lungs heaving, breathing air.

Still, white, winter world;
beneath, another, snugly furled.

Anticipating

Eggs
are opening;
hives
are opening;
dens
are opening;
doors
are opening;
wings
are opening;
eyes
are opening;
beaks
are opening;
jaws
are opening:
spring
is opening.

Summer
is waiting.

Busy Blackbird

Skids about the garden,
never stops to rest,
stuffing beak with shreds and bits –
never mind what's best.
Flaps off over tree-tops,
dropping stalks and sticks...
back again – more hops, more bits:
blackbird building nest.

Cocky Cock-Robin

Hoppy, flappy, happy little thing!
Bullies all the other birds:
thinks he's King.

Hide-and-Sleep

I dropped down in the high summer grass
and waited...

gazing up at daydream-blue
through elf-and-pixie-green;
finger-tipping the fringe-tipped stems
and crumbling them up with my thumb;
floating away on their sugar-puffed scent,
lulled by a bee's dull hum;
dozing in my meadow-bed
behind my fairy screen...

till a head popped through
and my friend said *Boo!*
And so did I.

Sunny Sunday in the Park

Sunshine spangling, streaming,
lovers ambling, dreaming,
families chatting, strolling,
sportsmen batting, bowling,
toddlers staring, gazing,
parents sharing, praising,
kids rambling, scrambling, rolling, screaming,
larking round the park till dark.

Fox barking, barking.

What Sort of Green is a Sun-Lit Leaf?

A yellowy, mellowy, melt-away green:
a green with a sheen of queen's velveteen,
of a mermaid, of limeade, of lime marmalade,
of gold braid inlaid with gem-stones of jade.

A luscious, liquid, luminous green,
only seen in slivers and chinks in between,
through gaps and glades in summery scenes -
a sunshine-saturated shade of green,
miracle-made.

Birds Over Buildings

Glancing up at the sky
on my shopping trawl,
over the buses and bus stops and cranes and clocks
and houses and shops and towers and spires
and pylons and high-rise blocks,
I saw a **V** of tiny birds
curving.

V for Victory!
shone their shiny curve,
as they swerved over our sprawl.

Glad I'm not a Human

Glad I'm not a human, said the germ,
with me inside!

Glad I'm not a hippo, said the human,
five feet wide!

Glad I'm not a fish, said the hippo,
with no legs!

Glad I'm not a pig, said the fish,
with no eggs!

Glad I'm not a parrot, said the pig,
with no snout!

Glad I'm not a parrot, said the parrot,
but he didn't know what he was talking about.

Daydreaming

Lazing on dry sand,
gazing at high gulls,
holding golden days in my hand.

In My Next Life

I want to be a tree, says Marie
(she's three).

I want to be a shark, says Mark
(he's six).

I want to be a swan, says Yvonne
(she's eight).

I want to be me, says me
(I'm nine).

I want to be an orang-utan, says Dad
(he's thirty-nine),
and swing about in the jungle twine
going Oo-oo-oo! all the time.

You want your head seen to, says Mum
(she's a hundred-and-nine sometimes).

Index of Creatures

Albatros	29
Ant	42
Badger	49
Bat	52
Bee	69
Blackbird	68
Butterfly	39
Camel	20
Crab	30
Creepy crawlies	35-48, 58, 69
Crocodile	12
Daddy-longlegs	45
Dolphin	26
Dragonfly	35
Duck	33
Elephant	15
Fish	27, 33, 73, 75
Fox	48, 54-56, 70
Frog	48
Giraffe	13
Gull	74
Hawk	57
Hedgehog	60
Heron	31
Hibernators	66
Hippopotamus	16, 73
Hyena	5
Jaguar	6
Jellyfish	30
Kangaroo	18
Ladybird	46
Leopard	4
Lion	4
Mayfly	48
Migrating birds	72
Mole	61
Monkey	1, 3, 75
Moth	47, 58
Mouse	48, 50
Owl	58
Parrot	8, 73
Penguin	23
Polar bear	21
Pony	64
Rabbit	56
Rat	51
Rhinoceros	16, 17
Robin	68
Slug	36-37
Snail	40
Snake	19
Spider	43
Squirrel	59
Swan	31
Tiger	9-11
Toad	48, 63
Walrus	22
Wasp	41
Whale	28
Wolf	53
Woodlouse	44
Worm	38
Zebra	14

Index of Weather & Whereabouts

Hot	1-20
Cold	21-24, 62-67
Watery	24-35
Muddy Mix	32-75

Riddle Answers

P.35 - Dragonflies
P.37 - Worm
P.52 - Bat
P.53 - Wolf
P.60 - Hedgehog